G

—

*the remarkable true story of
the world's most devoted terrier*

John Mackay

Lang**Syne**

PUBLISHING

WRITING *to* REMEMBER

Vineyard Business Centre,
Pathhead, Midlothian EH37 5XP
Tel: 01875 321 203 Fax: 01875 321 233
E-mail: info@lang-syne.co.uk
www.langsyneshop.co.uk

Design by Roy Boyd
Printed by Ricoh Print Scotland
First published 1994. Reprinted 1995, 1997 & 2004
© Lang Syne Publishers Ltd 2009

ISBN 978-1-85217-345-6

Greyfriars Bobby

Edinburgh, as with other cities, has had its dogs of distinction.

There was "Rab", a hero of the Victorian story '*Rab and his Friends*' by Edinburgh medical man Dr. John Brown.

And the little dog in Edinburgh Castle's military museum famed for chasing enemy cannon balls that had fallen short of their target, in battles fought more than one hundred years ago.

Nor must one forget the dog cemetery in that same fortress, resting place of regimental mascots.

As I write, looking across fields of the Scottish Border country, I see a descendant of the dog who had his brief moment of glory herding sheep on the Castle esplanade for his master 'Skipper' Gilchrist in a sequence some years ago at the Edinburgh Military Tattoo.

In the literary field, a fictitious dog entitled to be included here is '*The Hound of the Baskervilles*' who was created by Edinburgh-born author Sir Arthur Conan Doyle.

And Sir Walter Scott's favourite dog Maida is shown looking up to him in the Princes Street monument.

In Scott's '*Guy Mannering*' there is a character called Dandie Dinmont who gave his name, as the popularity of the novel became widespread, to his dog.

This was a breed like a Border terrier, a devoted little animal; a worker, shaggy-haired and courageous. Such a description fits well the most famous dog of all – Greyfriars Bobby – whose story is given here. As Walt Disney remarked when preparing his film on Bobby: *"This is one of the classical animal tales of the world"*.

Bobby comes to Edinburgh

Bobby's origin, and indeed even his breed, has been open to contradiction in the past.

One writer was quite adamant that Bobby was a Scotch terrier. But we can now safely settle for Skye terrier – perhaps with a mongrel strain – giving the toughness that stood him well, both in dealing with other dogs when he came to Town and during his long years of vigil.

He is first heard of as a puppy belonging to John Gray. Was Gray a farmer who came to Edinburgh to the fairs in the Grassmarket?

Or was he a shepherd, or some farmworker in the Lothians?

The latter is most likely for it is established that at some time in the early 1850s John Gray came to Edinburgh and joined the Police Force.

Then the force was still in its early years of authority and had much to contend with in the ill-lit streets of the Old Town and its shadowed wynds and closes.

Thus, while the New Town of Edinburgh across the valley to Princes Street flourished in its fresh found gentility and young Robert Louis Stevenson watched for the lamplighter in Heriot Row, John Gray patrolled in the slums of the Old Town, accompanied by Bobby.

These were the days of notable criminals. When Gray was a boy in the Lothians, Burke and Hare were pursuing their macabre trade in supplying bodies huddled in herring barrels to Surgeons' Square at £10 a time.

And David Haggart, aged twenty, born around the same time as Gray, was writing his autobiography in prison while awaiting his hanging. For *"there never was a riper scoundrel"*, observed Lord Cockburn.

One of the notable criminals of the time when Gray was considering exchanging country life for Town, was poisoner and bigamist William Bennison, a type of 'Holy Willie' with a habit of introducing arsenic into his wife's morning plate of porridge.

On the other side of the picture of that time, there were those working for the public good.

Dr. Thomas Guthrie, the famous minister, founded the 'Ragged Schools' where young lads were persuaded to come off the streets and attend classes, steering them away from the idleness that bred mischief; and in turn, crime.

Dr. Guthrie is the impressive figure with one of his 'pupils' in the statue in Princes Street, opposite South Castle Street. He was also a great preacher who could thunder from the pulpit to great effect. In one instance, calling on the congregation to save sinners, a young man on naval leave, overcome by the preacher's eloquence, sprang from his seat and threw off his jacket to take the plunge – until he realised where he was!

That happened in the church at the head of the Upper Bow in the Lawnmarket; by stepping down the

Upper Bow to its lower section, the West Bow (once the only entrance to Edinburgh from the west) and descending to the Grassmarket, then left, to the entrance to the Cowgate opposite the smaller gate to Greyfriars, one is on the stamping ground of Greyfriars Bobby himself.

When Gray came to Edinburgh with his family and dog he found lodging in the Cowgate which stretches now under the George IV Bridge and the South Bridge to the site of the gate through which the cows once went to pasture marking an eastern exit through the Old Town Wall.

The Cowgate, from being in its heyday an aristocratic thoroughfare with its gardens and orchards set on the southern facing slopes of the Old Town ridge, has changed through the years and become a street of contrasts.

In the Victorian era it was a rich hunting ground for the petty criminal. The policeman, often a target for the less friendly inclined, had at times need for a lively associate.

One for example, to give chase and get his teeth into the thief's breeches – if not one of his legs.

When his master had occasion, first, to attend the distressed and often elderly victim he kept a firm grip of the attacker.

Nor were the roaming strays – Edinburgh's army of homeless dogs – long in finding out that Bobby was better avoided.

Bobby and his master

Bobby goes to market

A near contemporary of John Gray (who would, by the time Gray was in the Force be writing of his life of hunting the criminal) was Detective James McLevy who also lived in the Cowgate at the foot of Old Fishmarket Close.

Unlike Gray, McLevy did not have a dog as a partner but was himself a tireless runner.

He describes in one of his books how he ran for over a mile after a thief *"with no abatement of the speed of either (pursuer and pursued) – a criminal may almost always be caught by loss of breath, fear eats up the energy, the lungs play violently and exhaustion is the consequence . . ."*

The Grassmarket, under the shadow of Edinburgh Castle was one of his patrolling grounds (previous to his promotion as detective) when McLevy was designated 'nightwatchman' – a role also taken over by John Gray with Bobby in attendance, of course.

This writer, as a lad, remembers seeing author Bailie Wilson McLaren who, in old age, described the Grassmarket as he remembered it in his youth. He gives a first hand impression of the fair there . . .

"The Fair was in full swing, crowds of young and old full of eager excitement surrounded the long line of barrows... the smell from flaring oil lamps did not disturb the appetites of those devouring toothsome ginger bread, sliced coconut and bloody (black)

puddings. The clamouring voices of hucksters trying to
dispose of wares mingles with those of keepers of
travelling booths..."

Bailie McLaren actually met Greyfriars Bobby
as will be described in his own words later.

Not only was the Grassmarket a place for fairs
but also a market dating from the 15th century and
spread over the huge area, as King James III decreed in
his granting of the charter – "from Greyfriars to the
westwards" (the western extremity of the Town Wall
whose upper reaches still show in part at the summit of
the Vennel, the passage way rising at the west end of the
Grassmarket).

In Bobby's day, hundreds of drovers brought
their wide-horned beasts from the Highlands while from
the Borders came shepherds with their flock.

On the night before the sales the Grassmarket
had to be patrolled by those appointed to observe that no
rustlers enticed an animal away from its snoring keeper
wrapped in his plaid by the pen.

Bobby would be particularly vigilant here.

The Highland drovers, with Queen Victoria's
encouragement again for the common man to wear the
tartan – albeit a plaid stained with sweat and snuff in
their case – were a hardy lot and still inclined to sport a
sword as well as a staff.

Borderers and Highlanders meeting did not
encourage a friendly calm.

Nor did the military on late leave from the

Bobby at the Grassmarket cattle fair

Castle, swaying from the tavern howffs with their doxies on their arm.

Linked with the Market were the booths, jugglers, card sharpers and as background, the White Hart Inn (where Robert Burns once stayed) contending with the arrival and departure of stagecoaches – and horses for sale showing their paces nearby.

After a spell of duty in the Grassmarket or Cowgate and other parts of the Old Town, it was John Gray's custom to walk up Candle-maker Row by Greyfriars, to the eating house at No. 6 Greyfriars Place.

There, dog and man would rest and refresh themselves.

Never would John Gray think that the little restaurant would in its way become famous because of a four-legged, non-paying 'customer'!

'Auld Jock' became John Gray's nickname. Perhaps a term of affection, for old he was not; nor was there any indication on his features of a premature ageing.

But eventually the ravages of the tuberculosis struck at John Gray.

Bad slum housing and the east winds that funnelled through the narrow closes and canyon-like thoroughfares when he was on duty in all weathers, did not help.

Policeman John Gray had eventually to be invalided out of the Force and after being confined to bed in his lodging in the Cowgate he died late in the winter of 1858.

Bobby begins his vigil

The funeral was attended by members of the Force and also by Bobby who walked in the doleful procession wending its way along the Cowgate and up the steep slope of Candlemaker Row.

Then, through the gateway to the churchyard of Greyfriars, the little procession turned to the right, going down the path a short way parallel with the backs of the houses of Candlemaker Row where, at the left side of this path, the grave had been prepared.

It is reasonable to suppose that Bobby would have to be restrained from some demonstration of his anxiety and bewilderment at this solemn ceremony.

John Gray's son may well have had to take him forcibly from the scene.

Indeed it may be that Bobby had not even been allowed to enter and had been kept back at the gate to Greyfriars for officially dogs were certainly not allowed in the churchyard.

That same night, as was customary when Bobby was off duty, he was let out of the house before the locking up for the night.

For, regardless of events, of a mourning household, dogs must be allowed their evening perambulation.

Not this time however, the stroll with his master.

Nor the usual nosing round the walls and the exploration of fascinating smells, for the small shaggy-

aired character headed straight along the Cowgate,
gnoring both canine friendly overtures or challenges to
ght.

Then up Candlemaker Row, a squirm under the
ate of Greyfriars and down the path sharp right to the
arthen mound by the grave.

And in the darkness, Bobby crouched there,
ose on paws.

Next morning he was discovered at his post and
hoo-ed off, but only with the greatest difficulty did the
ttendants succeed in getting him outside the gate and
oth the man in charge of the churchyard and the
ravedigger went back about their business.

Soon afterwards Bobby returned once more to
ettle, nose on paws, at the now completed earthen
1ound above John Gray's last resting place.

In time, the little
rrier, soon to be known as
ireyfriars Bobby, won. He
as allowed the occupation of
1e churchyard; not that his
igil meant a continual
ccupation of the graveside.

Winter weather had
be contended with.

Even dogs must
1elter – either under a
mbstone which happened to
e raised on short legs of stone

like a table next to the graveside or be persuaded to sta
the night at some friendly house nearby; and alway
there was the eating house in Greyfriars Place for foo
and warmth, now owned by a Mr Traill.

Before an account of Bobby's association wi
the Traills, some details on the church and churchyard c
Greyfriars.

The monastery of the Grey Friars, built mic
15th century, was originally occupied by a body c
Franciscans from Europe.

At first, they refused to be housed in th
building as they thought it too magnificent for the
needs, since they were vowed to a life of humility an
self denial and only agreed to occupy such sumptiou
lodgings on the plea of the Archbishop of St. Andrews

The monastery gave shelter to Royalty in i
time.

It was positioned in the present-day ang
formed by the south east end of the Grassmarket wi
the upward line of Candlemaker Row; and th
monastery gardens and orchard rose up the slope to t
south to where Lauriston Place is now.

At the time of the Reformation, the Edinburg
mob, led by the Earl of Argyle, began their work
desecration and destruction in the Town.

The monastery of the Grey Friars was one
the buildings most completely destroyed; and it w
after this that the officials of the Town were granted t
monastery grounds as a new burial place which today

widely known as containing one of the most impressive collections of tombstones and memorials in Britain.

John Gray shares his last resting place with a distinguished and sometimes notorious company, including the Regent Morton, ruler of Scotland, after Mary Queen of Scots' abdication; George Buchanan, historian and tutor to her son James VI; James Mylne the Royal Master Mason; George Watson, founder of Watson's College; James Craig, architect of Edinburgh's New Town; John Kay of caricature fame, Lord Provost William Creech, sometime Robert Burns's publisher; architect William Adam; and Gillespie Graham, creator of the high-spired kirk on Castlehill.

Nor must Judge 'Bloody' Mackenzie be omitted, whose fondness for passing sentence of execution earned him his nickname; and finally, another who should be a doubtful tenant of this 'God's acre' – Captain John Porteous of the Town Guard, who was hanged by the Edinburgh mob after ordering that demonstrating spectators at the execution of a smuggler were to be shot dead.

A church was once built in these former garden grounds and replaced in 1612 when the churchyard had been established by the 'Old Church' where the National Covenant was signed.

In the 1650s the church was desecrated, among other places in the Town, by Cromwell's troopers.

And some thirty years later, a thousand Covenanters were brought to Greyfriars as prisoners and

confined in a strip of the open churchyard for fiv
months.

Early in the eighteenth century, the 'New
Church' was built onto the west end of the 'Old Church
and each church, although under the same roo
interpreted their Protestant faith in a different way an
consequently each had their own minister.

Not until both Churches of Scotland united i
1928 was the dividing wall between the two places c
worship in the Greyfriars removed to become th
impressive single interior it is today.

Such was the historic ground on whic
Greyfriars Bobby spent the next fourteen years of h
life.

Bobby becomes a star

As the years passed, so Bobby's fame spread abroad.

If all that had happened today, TV camer
would be in attendance and the newspapers would ha
a great story.

But in Bobby's time, the media w
represented only by a journalist or two, maybe a pione
photographer and most persistently, artists, keen
record this exceptional dog with pencil and brush.

Bobby is big news!

Nor was he ever short of food, for, apart from having become a regular customer at Traill's Eating House, many of his callers brought him some tit-bits.

He even had night visitors in the person of the Law as represented by a policeman or two, on late duty who would find, of a summer's night when they were patrolling among the eerie silhouettes of tombstone and sepulchre, Bobby's face revealed in the rays of their lantern light, crouched by his master's grave.

Since he would recognise the uniform and top hat of the Force as a friend, the visit would be welcome and although the body snatching horror prevalent in Edinburgh not so very long ago would be nothing more than an unpleasant memory of the past, the little dog's presence, from the policemen's point of view, could be considered an advantage, for such a 'guard' although small in stature, was of a nature markedly aggressive and could discourage any interloper who would brave such a place in the dark.

In winter it was a different story and although Mr Traill tried to house the dog permanently, this was accepted only on a temporary basis when conditions outside were not fit for man or for beast.

This happy association between man and dog developed to an amusing situation with another of Bobby's friends and connected, of all things, with the one o'clock time gun from Edinburgh Castle.

The Castle is seen as an impressive backcloth from the churchyard grounds and prominent on the fortress is the Half Moon Battery from where the gun was fired.

The shot, especially when the north-west wind prevailed, was clearly heard in the churchyard and apparently Bobby began to associate the noise with, as it were, a dinner gong.

It happened that the little dog had become friends with a William Dow, a cabinet maker employed at nearby George Heriot's School from whose grounds a gateway opens into the churchyard, and it was Mr Dow's habit to come through this gateway and cross the churchyard to Mr Traill's Eating House for his dinner.

Since Bobby also had his dinner there, he and Dow became friends and thus the gunfire and appearance of the cabinet maker became associated with dinner time, to the extent that Mr Dow often found Bobby waiting for him at the school grounds' exit gateway – prompted by the one o'clock signal.

A note on the one o'clock gun may be of interest.

That a time gun should be introduced to Edinburgh was the suggestion of a city man who, on business in Paris, was intrigued by the time gun there which could be fired by the rays of the sun at mid-day.

Since the rays of the sun are not always prevalent in our northern fastness, it was decided that a time gun should be tried out and fired each day except Sunday, by an attendant artilleryman.

And many an elderly lady perambulating the

exclusive thoroughfare of Princes Street was treated to stimulating, albeit startling, shocks at odd times of the day when the gun was tried out from various points on the Castle battlements before a fixed time and place was settled upon.

The Half Moon Battery was eventually chosen and one o'clock as the best time, and it continued to fire from that position (apart from the war years) becoming first fired by electrical impulse in 1861.

During a performance at the closing stages of an evening showing of the Edinburgh Military Tattoo on the Castle esplanade, a muffled explosion was heard by the spectators.

No one was hurt but someone from a terrorist organisation had planted a device in the vicinity of the Half Moon Battery whose gun platform proved to have been weakened by the blast.

This incident happened some years ago and afterwards the military authorities decided to move the field gun used in firing the one o'clock signal, along with the full battery used in Royal salutes and so on, to the north facing position from where it now operates pointing across to Princes Street.

Bobby and his friends

It is an appropriate moment in Bobby's story to remark

on speculation once held that Bobby was the figment of a journalist's imagination.

This scribe, having been passing late at night by Greyfriars gateway, and desperate for a story against a deadline, saw a little dog a the gateway. This sight was enough to inspire the man to build up the story around that brief encounter.

It seems extraordinary now that at least one writer of high reputation and familiar with the Edinburgh scene joined in this theory.

This happened in the early 1930s when such mythical opinions appeared in the press.

Such opinions were emphatically quashed by letters to the newspapers by people who may well have never thought on library research. They had no need to, as proved by the following excerpts.

First, from a Mrs Meldrum: *"When I was a little girl I stroked Bobby and held him in my arms many times; my father* (the William Dow employed at Heriot's) *used the private path through Greyfriars."*

He was devoted to Bobby and we tried to coax him to our home but he would not leave the churchyard".

And a schoolboy of 1870 wrote in 1934 of how he left Heriot's at lunchtime to walk through the churchyard to Traill's Eating House – *"and every day a little dog came in for his dinner".*

About the same time in the 1930s Mr Traill's grand daughter wrote to say that – *"My mother often*

*told me that Bobby was by no means the picture of
dejection he is generally supposed to have been, but
often frightened her as a girl by fighting with other dogs
in Bristo and district".* (Bristo is the district now
covered by the University buildings to the north-east of
Greyfriars).

Finally on this theme of proving Bobby real, a
brief note from an account by Bailie Wilson McLaren
whom I quoted earlier.

He wrote that, in 1871, he frequented "Traill'
Coffee House in Greyfriars Place".

*"On one of my visits a Skye terrier was
chewing a bone. I gave the dog half of my buttered bap
(roll) and Mr Traill remarked that the dog has a bit of a
history.*

*"His name is Bobby and his master, named
Gray, died in 1858, almost thirteen years ago, and he
aye came for his dinner here and Bobby was always with
him".*

Bobby is arrested

By the time of Bailie McLaren's meeting with the little
dog, Bobby had been long established on the scene as "a
citizen of credit and renown" and a favourite with young
and old.

Thus, when some busybody brought to the

authorities' notice that Bobby's owner did not have a licence for the dog, the majesty of the Law summoned the populace.

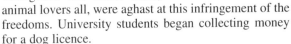

Who was Bobby's owner? His late master's family had vanished from the scene. Then surely it must be Mr Traill?

Bobby was "arrested". Youngsters and adults alike, animal lovers all, were aghast at this infringement of the freedoms. University students began collecting money for a dog licence.

"A very singular occurrence", wrote a report of the time, *"was brought to light in the Burgh Court... the hearing of a summons in regard to a dog tax. Proceedings were against a Mr Traill as owner"*.

However Mr Traill argued in Court that if he could claim the dog, he would certainly pay the tax, but as long as the dog refused to attach himself to anyone in particular, it was impossible to fix ownership.

This was agreed as logical by William Chambers, Lord Provost of Edinburgh, who brought matters to a satisfactory conclusion in the simplest of humanitarian ways by himself presenting Bobby later with an engraved collar with dog licence attached.

The collar can be seen today in the Huntly House Museum opposite the Tolbooth in the Canongate.

To have such a gift bestowed on him was surely the ultimate accolade for Bobby.

And it was a fitting end to his long and faithful vigil - Bobby died in the winter of 1872 at Mr Traill's home in Keir Street, the little thoroughfare leading off from Lauriston Place and just east of the Edinburgh College of Art.

Rumour persisted after Bobby's departure to the 'Happy Hunting Grounds' that his body was, secretly and at night, buried in an empty part of the churchyard.

Whether or not this is so, certainly he now has a stone there erected in his memory – the stone facing across to the entrance gateway and inscribed:

Greyfriars Bobby
Died 14th January 1872
Aged 16 Years

Let his Loyalty and Devotion
Be a Lesson to us all

Erected by the Dog Aid Society
of Scotland and Unveiled by H/R.H
The Duke of Gloucester G. C. V. O.
On 13th May 1981

If one then turns right to follow the path ranging with the rear of the Candlemaker Row houses, a few yards down that path and on the left there is another memorial stone.

This one is clustered in evergreen. The inscription reads:

> ***John Gray***
> ***Died 1858***
> ***'Auld Jock'***
> ***Master of 'Greyfriars Bobby'***
>
> ***"And Even In His Ashes***
> ***Most Beloved"***
>
> ***Erected by***
> ***American Lovers of Bobby***

The best known memorial to Bobby is, of course, the little statue surmounting what was once, appropriately, a drinking fountain for dogs at the head of Candlemaker Row where it joins with George IV Bridge.

It was modelled by William Brodie, the Royal Scottish Academician.

He is also noted as the sculptor of Sir James Y. Simpson, pioneer in the use of chloroform, who is shown solemnly seated at the extreme west end of West Princes Street Gardens just behind the pavement of the Street.

This and other larger works of Brodie's, and indeed most of the impressive array of Edinburgh's statuary, take second place in public interest to the modest little statue at the head of Candlemaker Row.

It had a Greek inscription by the famed

Professor Blackie of Edinburgh University which, translated, reads:

"This monument was erected by a noble lady, the Baroness Burdett Coutts, to the memory of Greyfriars Bobby, a faithful and affectionate little dog who followed the remains of his beloved master to the churchyard in 1858 and became a constant visitor to the grave, refusing to be separated from the spot until he died in 1872".

Bobby at the movies

So ends the story of Greyfriars Bobby.

However, a revival of interest in these events of Edinburgh's Victorian days arose, for some reason, after the Second World War and became concentrated in the glamorous world of the cinema.

Metro Goldwyn Mayer's roaring lion first introduced Bobby's story to the silver screen.

With a fine disregard for accuracy in the cause of the importance of the box office pull of star quality, the famed 'Lassie' star collie dog of MGM took the principal role, while her four months old son, Yip Yip, was cast to perform in the early sequences.

But to introduce some touch of authenticity to the proceedings, Ross, a Scottish Border collie was brought to Hollywood to instruct 'Lassie' in the finer points of herding sheep.

Here is part of the advance publicity:

"The story centres around the stray dog and his unofficial owner, beloved of the entire city of Edinburgh in the 1850s.

"Ownerless, the dog became the centre of a Law trial which attracted worldwide attention, particularly in the United States.

"A statue to his honour was erected by the dog's American admirers and still stands at Greyfriars cemetry, resting place of many of Scotland's heroes".

It may be that the idea of a film was initially

Walt Disney with his star – Bobby!

prompted by the fact that these years were around the centenary of Bobby's master's death.

But whatever was the initial inspiration, some years later Walt Disney got much nearer to the truth in his film version of the story.

He came to Edinburgh to look over the ground and consider, among many of his other problems, how to find a suitable dog to take Bobby's role.

Here, from news cuttings of that time, are references to the animals chosen and who trained them.

Disney's scouts discovered the ideal, it was thought, in a Skye terrier from the island of Lewis in the Hebrides, in one instance.

From another source it was reported that a Mr John Holmes was commissioned to find a film Bobby.

Holmes was a professional dog trainer for the film industry and the author of books on dogs.

A further report mentions a Mr John Daryls, a "world famed dog trainer" who was instrumental in bringing "ten stagestruck Skye terriers" all the way from the Island of Lewis to the film studios at Shepperton near London.

And which of these training gentlemen was the one reported to have taken part in the scene of the actual funeral procession?

He was inside the coffin, that being a suitable but unsighted position from where to keep the star dog controlled ensuring that it kept the required solemn pace for the camera.

Thus from the coffin came the instructions: *"Slow now, me boy... slow, slow..."*

Certainly one of the reported Skye terriers was photographed with Walt Disney and the same dog appeared at the world premiere in Edinburgh.

And it was there that the Press photographed, in the words of the publicity man, *"the £20,000 Highland trained dog in a £2,000,000 film"*.

The Disney blurb for the film declared:

"The story of the wee Skye terrier with the great big heart.

It actually happened!

It was photographed where it happened!

You'll have to see it to believe it!"

And now that all such ballyhoo has long subsided, thoughts turn again to the heart of it all... to the peace of the churchyard of Greyfriars, its ancient green sward surrounding that historic place of worship; and in that withdrawn sanctuary, it is not too difficult to imagine a little dog trotting across the grass to crouch once more, on guard, at his master's grave.

THE END